A Glimpse
at the
Way of the
Companions

by
Shaykh 'Abdul-Qaadir al-Arna'oot

Translated by
Abu Taher

ISBN 1 898649 05 7

British Library Cataloguing in Publication Data.
A catalogue record for this book is available from the British Library.

First Edition, 1415 AH/1994 CE

© Copyright 1994 by Al-Hidaayah Publishing & Distribution

Typeset by: Al-Hidaayah Publishing & Distribution

Cover design by: Abu Yahya Saleem

Published by: Al-Hidaayah Publishing & Distribution
                 P.O. Box 3332
                 Birmingham
                 United Kingdom
                 B10 9AW

                 Tel: 0121 753 1889
                 Fax: 0121 753 2422

Printed by: ALL TRADE PRINTERS (B'ham).

Contents

بِسْمِ اللَّهِ الرَّحْمَٰنِ الرَّحِيمِ

Translator's Introduction

All praise is for Allaah, we praise Him, seek His aid and ask for His forgiveness. We seek refuge in Allaah from the evil of ourselves and the evil of our actions. He whom Allaah guides then there is none who can misguide him, and he whom Allaah misguides then there is none who can guide him. I bear witness that none has the right to be worshipped (in truth) except Allaah alone, having no partners and I bear witness that Muhammad (ﷺ), is His slave and Messenger.

To proceed:

This is an abridgement of a small treatise written by the renowned scholar Shaykh 'Abdul-Qaadir al-Arna'oot (hafidhahullaah) who has specialised in the field of Hadeeth. His most famous works include the checkings of Zaadul M'aad by Ibn al-Qayyim, Jaami'-ul-Usool by Ibn al-Atheer and al-Adhkaar by Imaam an-Nawawee.

This is the first treatise in a series regarding the Methodology of the Prophet (ﷺ) and his Companions (may Allaah be pleased with them). It is the Methodology that was implemented by the Prophet (ﷺ) and adhered to by the best of generations (the Companions), giving them success in this world and ultimate success in the Hereafter. The series is entitled Tasfiyah wat Tarbiyah,* which are the two main instruments of this Prophetic Methodology that can be used to help us to remain firmly established upon the Deen of Islaam.

This treatise was written by Shaykh 'Abdul-Qaadir in response to the numerous questions that were posed to him and the general confusion

---

* Tasfiyah wat Tarbiyah: Restoration of the Deen to its original pure form as it was revealed to the Prophet (ﷺ) by removal and rejection of false beliefs, innovated practices and the fabricated and unauthentic ahaadeeth introduced into it (tasfiyah).
Educating and cultivating the Muslims upon this pure Deen so that their beliefs, worship and manners become those that were taught by the Prophet (ﷺ) and held and practised by the Companions (tarbiyah). (Publisher's note)

concerning this important matter. In compiling this treatise the Shaykh relied upon classical works, due to the importance of returning to the understanding of the early scholars of this *Ummah*.

The treatise has been translated in an attempt to remove the confusion surrounding this crucial subject, concerning the methodology adopted by the Prophet (ﷺ), and his Companions *(radiyallaahu 'anhum)*, in establishing Islaam as a way of life.

Every Muslim desiring to return to Islaam in its true sense, must grasp what the Prophet (ﷺ) and his Companions were upon, in all aspects of life. Only then can we move further towards establishing Islaam as our way of life.

This treatise highlights the main principles governing the correct understanding of this topic, following the way of the early scholars in clarifying and expounding the Prophetic Methodology.

The treatise has been abridged in order to remove some of the unnecessary technical terms, and also wherever necessary, clarification of some terms and points have been included. A glossary has also been added to assist the reader.

We praise Allaah and ask Him to make this treatise beneficial to the Muslims and to guide us to the Straight Path, the Path of the Prophet (ﷺ) and his Companions. We ask Allaah to make this purely for His Face for verily He is All-Hearing, All-Knowing.

Abu Taher

A GLIMPSE AT THE WAY OF THE COMPANIONS

Definition of *Manhaj*

Linguistically and in the *Sharee'ah*: *An-nahju, al-manhaj* and *al-minhaaj* mean the clear and manifest way. Allaah the Most High says in the glorious Qur'aan:

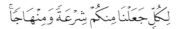

To each among you we have prescribed a law and a *minhaaj*
[al-Maa'idah (5):48]

Meaning a law and a way which is clearly explained. Indeed Allaah, the Most High, prescribed for every nation a law and a clear way (a *manhaj*). Thus the people of the Tauraat had a law and the people of the Injeel had a law and the people of the Qur'aan have a law.

These laws differ in their rules (*ahkaam*) but are united in the *tawheed* of Allaah (uniqueness of Allaah) as Allaah's Messenger (ﷺ) said:

"I am the most worthy person to 'Eesa Ibn Maryam in this world and the Hereafter. The Prophets are paternal brothers, their mothers are different, and their Deen is one. There is no Prophet between 'Eesa and myself."[1]

The meaning of this is that they (the prophets) are united upon the fundamentals of uniqueness (*tawheed*) of Allaah; as for the branches (*furoo'*) of law and legislation, then differences occurred in them. Thus their laws are different.

Allaah the Most High says:

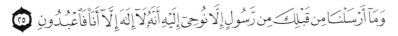

---

1. Reported by al-Bukhaaree in his *Saheeh*, the Book of Prophets, chapter 'Remember the Book of Maryam', Muslim in his *Saheeh* (no. 2365), the Book of Merits, chapter 'Merits of 'Eesa peace be upon him'. From the *hadeeth* of Aboo Hurairah (*radiyallaahu 'anhu*).

And we did not send any Messenger before you (O Muhammad) but we inspired to him that (say) There is none who has the right to be worshipped except I (Allaah), so worship Me (alone and none else).
[al-Anbiyaa' (21):25]

Also, the Saying of Allaah the Most High:

And verily, We have sent among every nation (*Ummah*) a Messenger proclaiming: Worship Allaah alone and avoid the *Taaghoot* (all false deities).
[an-Nahl (16):36]

This is in respect of *tawheed* (oneness) of Allaah, the One free from all defects. As for the laws, then they differed with respect to the commands and prohibitions.

Linguistic[2] and legal definition of the word *Salaf*

1) *As-Salaf* - That which has past and preceded. Hence it is said *Salafa shai Salafan* to mean something has passed; *Salafa fulanan Salafan* to mean someone has preceded; *as-saalif* - a predecessor; *as-salaf* - a group of predecessors, and *as-salaf* - a people who have preceded us in conduct.

Allaah says:

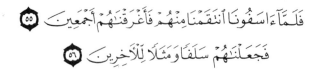

---

2. The linguistic definitions of the word *Salaf* are many; here the author has mentioned a few of them. (Translator)

So when they angered Us we punished them, and drowned them all, and made them a precedent - Salafan (as a lesson for those coming after them) and an example to later generations.
[az-Zukhruf (43):55-56]

That is *"when they angered Us We punished them, drowning them all making them a precedent,"* predecessors for those who do actions like theirs, so that the people coming after them can take heed and warn others by their example.

2) *As-Salaf:* Every good deed that one does. It is said: *Qad salaf lahu amal saalih* meaning, verily he has good deeds that have preceded him.

3) *As-Salaf:* Those who precede you, from amongst your forefathers and relatives, who may be older than you or better than you in merit.[3] The singular of this term is *Saalif.*

Due to this the first generation (the Companions) were called *as-Salaf as-Saalih* (the Pious Predecessors).

The Messenger of Allaah (ﷺ) and his Companions and those that follow them in *Ihsaan*[4] are the *Salaf* of this *Ummah*.[5]

---

3. This definition can be found in *Lisaan ul-Arab,* by Ibn Mandhoor al-Afreeqee. (Translator)

4. *Ihsaan,* in this usage has been explained to mean following in terms of beliefs, sayings and actions. Refer to *Tayseer al-Kareem ar-Rahmaan fee Tafseer Kalaamul-Mannaan,* the book of *Tafseer* by Shaykh 'Abdur-Rahmaan bin Naasir as-Sa'dee. (Translator)

5. The technical (Islamic) meaning of the word *Salaf,* as understood by the majority of the scholars of *Ahl-Sunnah wal-Jamaa'ah,* has been defined as being the Companions, the Successors (*taabi'oon*) and the Successors to the Successors (*atbaa at-taabi'oon*) that is the first three generations. This has been taken from the saying of the Prophet (ﷺ): *"The best of people are my generation then those who come after them, then those who come after them, then there will come a people in whom there will be no good."* Reported by at-Tabaraanee from Ibn Mas'ood and declared authentic by al-Albaanee in *Saheeh al-Jaami',* and there are many other similar *ahaadeeth* to the above, all of which have lead to the definition of the word *Salaf* being restricted to the first three generations. (Translator)

Matters concerning their Methodology

(i) Status of the Prophet (ﷺ)

Everyone who calls to what the Messenger of Allaah (ﷺ), his Companions and their successors called to, then he is upon the way of the *Salaf as-Saalih.* It is obligatory upon all the Muslims to follow the Noble Book (Qur'aan) and the pure *Sunnah*, by going back to the understanding of the Pious Predecessors (*Salaf as-Saalih*), may Allaah be pleased with them all. For verily they are the ones that deserve the most to be followed, as they were truthful in their faith, strong in their beliefs and sincere in their worship.

The leader (*Imaam*) of the *Salaf as-Saalih* is Allaah's Messenger, Muhammad (ﷺ), whom Allaah has ordered us, in His Book (the Qur'aan), to follow, in His saying:

$$وَمَآ ءَاتَىٰكُمُ ٱلرَّسُولُ فَخُذُوهُ وَمَا نَهَىٰكُمْ عَنْهُ فَٱنتَهُواْ$$

And whatsoever the Messenger (Muhammad) gives you take it, and whatsoever he forbids you abstain from it.
[al-Hashr (59):7]

The Prophet (ﷺ) is a beautiful example, and a righteous model to be followed, Allaah the Most High says:

$$لَّقَدْ كَانَ لَكُمْ فِى رَسُولِ ٱللَّهِ أُسْوَةٌ$$
$$حَسَنَةٌ لِّمَن كَانَ يَرْجُواْ ٱللَّهَ وَٱلْيَوْمَ ٱلْأَخِرَ وَذَكَرَ ٱللَّهَ كَثِيرًا ﴿٢١﴾$$

Indeed in the Messenger of Allaah (Muhammad) you have a good example to follow, for him who hopes in meeting Allaah and the Last Day and remembers Allaah much.
[al-Ahzaab (33):21]

The Prophet (ﷺ) is the one that speaks by revelation sent to him from the heavens:

Nor does he speak of his own desire. It is only an inspiration that
is inspired.
[an-Najm (53):3-4]

Allaah, the Most High, ordered that we judge by the Messenger (ﷺ) in all
affairs of our life. Allaah, the One free of all defects, says:

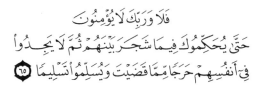

But no by your Lord, they can have no faith, until they make you
judge in all disputes between them, and find in themselves no
resistance against your decision and accept them with full
submission.
[an-Nisaa' (4):65]

Allaah, the Most High, warned us about opposing the Prophet (ﷺ) saying:

So let those who oppose the Messenger's commandments (i.e. his
Sunnah) beware lest some *fitnah* (disbelief, trials, afflictions,
earthquakes, killing, overpowered by a tyrant, etc.) befall them or
a painful torment be inflicted on them.
[an-Noor (24):63]

The reference point of the *Salaf*, whenever they have a disagreement, is the
Book of Allaah, the Mighty and Majestic, and the *Sunnah* of the Messenger
(ﷺ).

Allaah ,the Most High, says:

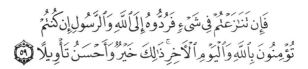

And if you differ in anything amongst yourselves refer it to Allaah and his Messenger, if you believe in Allaah and in the Last Day. That is better and more suitable for final determination.
[an-Nisaa' (4):59]

The Messenger of Allaah (ﷺ) is the conveyer (of news) from his Lord and the one who explains His Book. Allaah the Most High says:

$$وَأَنزَلْنَاۤ إِلَيْكَ ٱلذِّكْرَ لِتُبَيِّنَ لِلنَّاسِ مَا نُزِّلَ إِلَيْهِمْ$$

And we have sent down to you (Muhammad) the reminder and the advice (the Qur'aan) that you may explain clearly to men what is sent down to them.
[an-Nahl (16):44]

The Messenger (ﷺ) said in a *hadeeth*:

"Adhere to my Sunnah and the Sunnah of the rightly guided Khulafaa', bite on to it with your molar teeth and beware of newly invented matters, for verily every innovation (bid'ah) is a going astray."[6]

---

6. Reported by Ahmad bin Hanbal in *Musnad* (4/126, 127), Aboo Daawood in his *Sunan* (4607) in the Book of *Sunnah*, chapter 'Adhering to the *Sunnah*', at-Tirmidhee in his *Sunan* (no.2678) in the Book of Knowledge, Chapter '16', Ibn Majah, in his *Sunan* (no.42) in the *Muqaddimah* (introduction) and others. From the *hadeeth* of 'Irbaad bin Saariyah (*radiyallaahu 'anhu*), and it is an authentic *hadeeth*. Refer to the detailed explanation of the *hadeeth* in *Jaami' al-Uloom wal-Hikaam* by Haafidh Ibn Rajab al-Hanbalee (*rahimahullaah*), for verily he has done extremely well in explaining it and benefited others in doing so.

(ii) Status of the Companions

The best of the *Salaf* after the Messenger of Allaah (ﷺ) are the Companions, who took their Religion (*Deen*) from the Messenger (ﷺ) with truthfulness and sincerity; just as Allaah has described them in His Book when He said:

مِّنَ ٱلۡمُؤۡمِنِينَ رِجَالٌ صَدَقُواْ مَا عَٰهَدُواْ ٱللَّهَ عَلَيۡهِ فَمِنۡهُم مَّن قَضَىٰ نَحۡبَهُۥ وَمِنۡهُم مَّن يَنتَظِرُ وَمَا بَدَّلُواْ تَبۡدِيلًا ۝

Among the believers are men who have been true to their covenant with Allaah and showed not their backs to the disbelievers, of them some have fulfilled their obligations and some of them are still waiting, but they never changed (i.e. they never proved treacherous to their covenant which they concluded with Allaah) in the least.
[al-Ahzaab (33):23]

They are the ones who did righteous deeds, which Allaah, the Most High, has mentioned in His Book; in His saying:

وَلَٰكِنَّ ٱلۡبِرَّ مَنۡ ءَامَنَ بِٱللَّهِ وَٱلۡيَوۡمِ ٱلۡأٓخِرِ وَٱلۡمَلَٰٓئِكَةِ وَٱلۡكِتَٰبِ وَٱلنَّبِيِّۧنَ وَءَاتَى ٱلۡمَالَ عَلَىٰ حُبِّهِۦ ذَوِى ٱلۡقُرۡبَىٰ وَٱلۡيَتَٰمَىٰ وَٱلۡمَسَٰكِينَ وَٱبۡنَ ٱلسَّبِيلِ وَٱلسَّآئِلِينَ وَفِى ٱلرِّقَابِ وَأَقَامَ ٱلصَّلَوٰةَ وَءَاتَى ٱلزَّكَوٰةَ وَٱلۡمُوفُونَ بِعَهۡدِهِمۡ إِذَا عَٰهَدُواْ وَٱلصَّٰبِرِينَ فِى ٱلۡبَأۡسَآءِ وَٱلضَّرَّآءِ وَحِينَ ٱلۡبَأۡسِ أُوْلَٰٓئِكَ ٱلَّذِينَ صَدَقُواْ وَأُوْلَٰٓئِكَ هُمُ ٱلۡمُتَّقُونَ ۝

But Righteousness is the quality of one who believes in Allaah, the Last Day, the Angels, the Book, the Prophets and gives his wealth, in spite of love for it, to the relative, to the orphans and to the poor who beg and to the wayfarer and to those who ask

and to set slaves free, and offers the prayer perfectly (*iqamat-as-Salat*), and gives the *zakat* (obligatory charity) and who fulfil their covenant when they make it, and who are patient in extreme poverty and ailment (disease) and at the time of fighting (during battles); such are the people of the truth and they are the pious. [al-Baqarah (2):177]

This verse is the verse which professes the truth with which the Companions have been described with.

Sources of the *Deen*

The Book of Allaah, the Most High, is their manual (*dustoor*) and their law then the *Sunnah* after[7] the Book of Allaah. The *Sunnah* is the most blessed of sources and the best of sciences, the most beneficial of all, in the *Deen* and *Dunyah* (world), after the Book of Allaah, the One free of all defects. It is like the meadows and gardens, you find in it all goodness and righteousness. After the *Sunnah*, their manual is that which the *Salaf* of this *Ummah* and it's *A'immah* have agreed upon.

The *Salaf as-Saalih* are also: The Best Generation, about which the Messenger of Allaah (ﷺ) said in a *hadeeth*:

---

7. The majority of the scholars of *Ahl-Sunnah* say that the Qur'aan and the *Sunnah* go hand in hand, not one before the other. One does not refer to the *Sunnah* only when nothing is found in the Qur'aan. Rather whenever one needs to look for a verdict one goes back to the Qur'aan and *Sunnah*, together. Shaykh al-Albaanee, in *Silsilat-ul-Ahaadeeth ad-Da'eefah* (vol 2 no.881), says: "... rather it is obligatory to refer to the Book and *Sunnah*, together, without differentiating between them, since the *Sunnah* explains the general (*mujmal*) verses of the Qur'aan, restricts its unrestricted verses, specifies its general verses, as is known..."

There are many sayings from the *Salaf* showing that this view was held by them. Imaam al-Awzaa'ee and Imaam Yahya bin Katheer and others have said: "The Qur'aan is in more need of the *Sunnah* than the *Sunnah* is of the Book. The *Sunnah* is *Qaadiatun* (conclusive) over the Book and the Book is not conclusive over the *Sunnah*." Reported by ad-Daarimee (1/117). Similar narrations from the *Salaf* concerning this topic can be found in the books of the *Salaf* like *al-Ibaanah* by Ibn Battah. (Translator).

"The best of the people are my generation, then those after them, then those after them..." and he (ﷺ) said: "..Then there will come a people giving witness when they are not asked to give witness. They will be dishonest and not be trusted. They will take vows but will not fulfil them. Fatness will appear amongst them."[8]

From their beliefs...

Thus the fundamentals of the Religion (*Usool ud-Deen*) which were adhered to by those that preceded from the leaders (*a'immah*) of the *Deen*, the scholars of the Muslims and the *Salaf as-Saalih* and what they called people to are:

That they believe in the Book and *Sunnah*;[9] the general and the detailed aspects of it. They attest to the oneness of Allaah the Mighty and Majestic, and attest to the Messengership of Muhammad (ﷺ).

They know their Lord by the attributes (*sifaat*) that His revelation has spoken of, or are attested to by the Messenger of Allaah (ﷺ) from that which is found in authentic *ahaadeeth*, narrated from him by just and reliable narrators.

---

8. Reported by al-Bukhaaree (5/190) in the book of Witness, chapter 'Do not be a witness to injustice if asked that,' and in the book of Merits of the Companions of the Prophet, chapter 'Merits of the Companions of the Prophet', and in the book of Softening the Hearts, chapter 'Warning regarding worldly pleasures, amusements and competing with each other for the enjoyment thereof' Muslim (no. 2535) in the book of Merits of the Companions, chapter 'Merits of the Companions then those after them then those after them' at-Tirmidhee (no. 2222) in the book of Trials, chapter 'That which has come regarding the first three generations' and (no.2303) in the book of Witness, chapter 'Best generations.' Aboo Daawood (no. 4657) in the book of *Sunnah*, chapter 'Merits of the Companions of the Messenger.' An-Nasaa'ee (7/17,18) in the book of Covenants and Vows, chapter 'Fulfilling Vows' all from the *hadeeth* of 'Imraan bin Hussain. Also reported by al-Bukhaaree (5/191) in the book of Witness, chapter 'Do not be a witness to injustice if asked to do that', the book of Merits of the Companions of the Prophet, chapter 'Merits of the Companions of the Prophet,' and in the book of softening the heart, chapter 'Covenants and Vows'. Muslim (no. 2533) in the book of Merits of the Companions of the Prophet. At-Tirmidhee (no.3858) in the book of virtues. All from the *hadeeth* of 'Abdullaah ibn Mas'ood *(radiyallaahu 'anhu)*.

9. This includes all authentic *hadeeth*, whether it be a narration with numerous chains (*mutawaatir*) or a *hadeeth* with just one, two or three chains (*ahaad*). The beliefs are based upon both, refer to the book by Abul Qaasim al-Asbahaanee *al- Hujjah fee Bayaan al-Mahajjah wa Sharh 'Aqeedatul Ahl-Sunnah*, ar-Risalaah by Imaam ash-Shaafi'ee and *Mukhtasar Sawaa'iqul Mursalah* by Ibn al-Qayyim. (Translator)

They affirm for Allaah, the Most High, that which He affirmed for Himself in His Book, or upon the tongue of His Messenger (ﷺ) without making Tashbeeh[10] (resembling) to His creation, without Tahreef (changing), without Tabdeel and without Tamtheel.[11]

Allaah, the Most High, says:

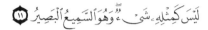

There is nothing like unto Him, and He is the all Hearer, all Seer.
[ash-Shoora (42):11]

---

10. *Tashbeeh: Tamtheel* (resembling, comparing) the *Sifaat* (attributes) of Allaah to the *sifaat* (attributes) of creation; "so it is not said that the Essence of Allaah is like our essence neither does it resemble our essence and likewise the *Sifaat* of Allaah - we do not say that His attributes are like our attributes, nor resemble our attributes. Rather it is *waajib* (obligatory) for a believer to stick to the saying of Allaah: **"There is nothing like unto Him.."** (ash-Shoora 42:11).

Tahreef: Changing the 'terms' of the names and attributes of Allaah or changing their 'meanings'; like the saying of the Jahmiyyah (a deviant sect) that *istawaa* (being high above the throne) means *istawlaa* (seizing power over something). Thus *Ahlus-Sunnah* do not do this.

Tabdeel: see *tahreef.*

Tamtheel: see *tashbeeh.*

Refer to *Tambihaat al-Laatifah 'alaa 'Aqeedatul-Waasitiyyah* by Shaykh Sa'dee (*rahimahullaah*). [Translator]

11. Shaykh-ul-Islaam Ibn Taymiyyah says in *'Aqeedatul-Waasitiyyah* when talking about *eemaan* (belief) in Allaah's *Sifaat* (attributes): "*Eemaan* (belief) in all what Allaah has described Himself by, in His Book and in what His Messenger Muhammad (ﷺ) has described Him by - without doing *tahreef, ta'teel, takyeef* or *tamtheel.*"

This statement shows two other principles held by *Ahl-Sunnah wal-Jamaa'ah* regarding *eemaan* in Allaah and His *Sifaat* (attributes); that is they do not do *Ta'teel*, which is to deny or reject the *Sifaat* of Allaah; and *takyeef* - which is to ask how and question their manner.

Refer to *'Aqeedatul-Waasitiyyah* by Ibn Taymiyyah, and *Qatful-Thamr fee-Bayaan 'Aqeedatul Ahlul-Athar* by Siddeeq Hasan Khaan, *Mukhtasar Sawaa'iqul-Mursalah* by Ibn al-Qayyim and *Fataawa al-Hamawiyyah al-Kubrah* by Ibn Taymiyyah.(Translator)

Imaam az-Zuhree[12] said: "Upon Allaah is the *bayaan* (explaining), upon the Messenger is the *balaagh* (conveying) and upon us is *tasleem* (willingly accepting)."[13]

Imaam Sufyaan bin 'Uyaynah[14] said: "All that Allaah has described Himself with in His Book, then its *tafseer* (explanation) is its reciting and keeping silent about it."

Imaam ash-Shaafi'ee[15] said: "I believe in Allaah, and that which has come from Allaah, upon the intended meaning of Allaah. I believe in the Messenger of Allaah (ﷺ) and that which has come from the Messenger of Allaah upon the intended meaning of the Messenger of Allaah (ﷺ)."

The *Salaf* and leaders of the *khalaf* (those later generations after the *Salaf*) may Allaah be pleased with them, proceeded along this way. They are all agreed upon, affirming, asserting and confirming that which is found in the Book of Allaah, the Most High, and the *Sunnah* of His Messenger (ﷺ), regarding Allaah's attributes without subjecting them to interpretation (*ta'weel*).

Verily we have been ordered to follow their way and to be guided by their light. The Messenger of Allaah (ﷺ) has warned us of newly invented matters, and informed us that they are from misguidance. He said in a *hadeeth*:

---

12. Muhammad bin Muslim bin 'Ubaidallah bin 'Abdullaah bin Shihaab bin Zahrah, Aboo Bakr. A *faqeeh* (jurist) and *haafidh*. His high status of proficiency is agreed upon. He is a successor, from Madeenah and one of the great Imaams, a scholar of the Hijaaz and Shaam. He died in 125H.

13. This is reported by al-Bukhaaree in *mu'allaq* form (13/503), by Ibn Abee Aasim in *Kitaab al-Adaab* and in *Kitaab az-Zuhd* (71) and by Aboo Nu'aym in *Hilyah* (3/179).

14. Sufyaan bin 'Uyaynah, Haafidh Aboo Muhammed al-Hilaalee al-Koofee. He was an *imaam*, a *haafidh*, a proof (*hujja*), having immense knowledge, and of great ability. A *muhaddith* (scholar of *hadeeth*) of the Haram of Makkah. Imaam ash-Shaafi'ee said about him: "Were it not for Maalik and Sufyaan the knowledge would have disappeared from the Hijaaz." He died whilst in Makkah in the year 198 hijree.

15. Muhammad bin Idrees bin al-'Abbaas bin Uthmaan bin Shoafa ash-Shaafi'ee al-Muttalibi; Aboo 'Abdullaah. He was a *mujaddid* (reviver) of the *Deen* at the beginning of 200 Hijree, a well known *imaam*. He died in Egypt in the year 204 Hijree.

"Adhere to my Sunnah (way) and to the Sunnah of the rightly guided Khulafaa'. Bite on to it with your molar teeth, and beware of newly invented matters, for verily every bid'ah (innovation) is a going astray." Its reference (takhreej) has preceded (see footnote no. 6).

'Abdullaah bin Mas'ood[16] (radiyallaahu 'anhumaa) said: "Follow and do not innovate for verily you have been sufficed."

'Umar bin 'Abdul 'Azeez[17] said "Do not go beyond where they stopped. For verily they stopped upon knowledge and with a perceiving view sufficed."

Imaam al-Awzaa'ee[18] said: "Stick to the footsteps of the Salaf, even if people abandon you. Beware of the views of men, even if they beautify it for you with words."

From the 'aqeedah[19] (beliefs) of the Salaf as-Saalih is their saying: Eemaan is a saying of the tongue, an action by the limbs and a strong belief in the heart. Eemaan increases with obedience to Allaah and decreases with disobedience to Allaah.

---

16. 'Abdullaah bin Mas'ood ibn Ghaafil ibn Habeeb al-Huthalee, Aboo 'Abdur-Rahmaan. From the first generation of Muslims and from the major Companions in merit and intellect. He migrated to Habasha (Ethiopia) and then to Madeenah. He witnessed the battle of Badr, Uhud, Khandaq, the pledge of Ridwaan and the remaining incidents with the Prophet (ﷺ); he was from the fuqahaa (jurists) of the Companions - may Allaah be pleased with them - he died in Madeenah in 32 hijree.

17. Aboo Hafs, 'Umar bin 'Abdul-Azeez bin Marwaan bin Hakam al-Amawee al-Qurashee. A righteous Khaleefah. Born and raised in Madeenatul-Munawwarah. He took the position of Khaleefah in the year 99 Hijree and died in the land of Shaam, in the year 101 Hijree.

18. 'Abdur-Rahmaan bin 'Amr bin Yuhmid al-Awzaa'ee. A famous Imaam of Syria. He used to live in Damascus, outside Bab al-Fraadees and then moved to Beirut and lived there, posted in the way of Allaah, until he died in the year 157 Hijree.

19. The word 'aqeedah signifies the things that one believes in (has eemaan in), hence the two words('aqeedah and eemaan) are sometimes synonymous. The word 'aqeedah being taking from the Arabic root of 'aqada - to tie - or fasten. Thus 'aqeedah is those things that the heart is tied to or fastened to, worshipping Allaah by it and, getting closer to Allaah. Refer to classical Arabic dictionaries like Lisaan ul-Arab by Ibn Mandhoor al-Afreeqee. (Translator)

From the beliefs of the *Salaf* is that good and evil is by the *Qadaa* (decree) of Allaah the Most High and His *Qadr* (pre-estimation). However evil is not ordered by Allaah, as some of them say: "All of it is ordered by Allaah," since Allaah has ordered good and prohibited evil. He did not order us with abominable acts, indeed He prohibited us from them. The human is not forced, he chooses his acts and beliefs. He deserves punishment or reward, depending upon his choice and he is the chooser in (doing or leaving) the ordered and prohibited things.

Allaah, the Most High, Says:

فَمَن شَآءَ فَلْيُؤْمِن وَمَن شَآءَ فَلْيَكْفُرْ

Then whosoever wills let him believe, and whosoever wills let him disbelieve.

[al-Kahf (18):29]

From the beliefs of the *Salaf* is that they do not make *takfeer*[20] of anyone of the Muslims due to a sin, even if it is from the major sins. Except if he denies (rejects) a thing that is known in the religion by necessity and is known by the scholars as well as the generality of people, and is based firmly upon the Book and the *Sunnah* and Consensus (*Ijmaa'*) of the *Salaf* of this *Ummah* and its leaders.

From the beliefs of the *Salaf as-Saalih* is that they worship Allaah, the Most High, and do not associate anything with Him. Thus they do not ask any one except Allaah, the Most High, of a need no one else can satisfy. They do not seek help (in which no one can help) from anyone except Allaah, the One free of all defects. They do not call upon anyone for aid (for an immediate need that no one can fulfil) except upon Allaah. They do not make *tawassul* (seeking nearness) to Allaah except by obeying Him, worshipping Him and doing good/righteous deeds.

---

20. *Takfeer* is the action of declaring a Muslim to have left Islaam. This is left for the people of knowledge (*'ulamaa*) to do and it must be done following strict guidelines. Refer to the book *al-'Uzar bil-Jahal wa rad 'alaa bid'atut Takfeer (The Excuse of Ignorance and the Refutation of the Innovation of Takfeer)* by Ahmad Fareed. (Translator)

This being taken from His saying:

$$\text{يَـٰٓأَيُّهَا ٱلَّذِينَ ءَامَنُوا۟ ٱتَّقُوا۟ ٱللَّهَ وَٱبْتَغُوٓا۟ إِلَيْهِ ٱلْوَسِيلَةَ}$$

**O you who believe! Do your duty to Allaah and fear Him, seek
the means of approach to Him.**
[al-Maa'idah (5):35]

That is, draw close to Allaah by obedience to Him and by worship of Him.

From the beliefs of the *Salaf as-Saalih* is that Prayer (*Salaat*) behind all righteous people and sinners is permissible if the external nature of the prayer is correct.[21]

We do not certify with certainty for anyone, whoever he may be, of being in Paradise or in Hell; except whoever the Messenger of Allaah (ﷺ) testified for. However we hope Paradise for the righteous and fear Hell for the sinful.

We testify for the ten people given the glad tidings of *Jannah* (Paradise), that they will be in *Jannah* (Paradise); just as the Prophet (ﷺ) testified this for them. We testify, as being in *Jannah*, for everyone that the Prophet (ﷺ) testifies this for them. This is because the Prophet does not speak of his own desire. Indeed it is nothing but revelation revealed to him.

---

21. What is implied by the statement *if the external nature of the prayer is correct* is that all the pillars and obligatory actions of the prayer are enacted by the one leading the prayer. For example that he faces the Qiblah etc. (Translator)

We take the Companions of Allaah's Messenger (صلى الله عليه وسلم) as *awliyaa* (friends). We refrain from showing their defects[22] and that which happened between them. Their affair is with their Lord. We do not abuse anyone of the Companions. This is taken from the Prophet's (صلى الله عليه وسلم) saying:

"Let none of you abuse (slander) my Companions. For by Him in whose Hand is my life, if one of you spent (in the way of Allaah) the equivalent of mount Uhud in gold it would not reach a handful nor half a handful of what they spent."[23]

The Companions are not infallible from error. Infallibility is for Allaah, the Most High, and for His Messenger (صلى الله عليه وسلم) in conveying the message. Allaah, the Most High, has protected the collective *Ummah* from mistakes (and not individuals) as the Prophet (صلى الله عليه وسلم) said:

---

22. The proof for this is abundant, found in the books of *'aqeedah* and *hadeeth*, like the saying of the Prophet (صلى الله عليه وسلم), *"When my companions are mentioned then refrain."* Reported in *Hilyatul-Awliyaa* (4/108), at-Tabaraanee in *al-Kabeer* (2/78/2) from the *hadeeth* of Ibn Mas'ood *(radiyallaahu 'anhu)*. Also in *Kitaab Sharh-us-Sunnah* by Imaam al-Barbahaaree, point 104, "...and if you see a man criticising the Companions of the Prophet (صلى الله عليه وسلم) then know that he is a person of wicked speech and desires, since Allaah's Messenger (صلى الله عليه وسلم) said: *"When my Companions are mentioned then refrain."* Since the Prophet (صلى الله عليه وسلم) knew any slips they would make after his death yet still he did not speak about them except good and said: *"Leave my Companions for me. For by Him in whose Hand is my soul, if you were to spend the like of Uhud or of the mountains in gold, you would not reach their actions."* Do not discuss about their slips or their wars, nor of that which the knowledge of which escapes you, and do not hear from anyone who speaks it, since your heart will not remain safe and sound if you hear it."

Thus *Ahl-Sunnah wal-Jamaa'ah* do not talk about such things, knowing that Allaah has forgiven them (the Companions) their errors. (Translator)

23. Reported by al-Bukhaaree (7/27,28) in the book of Merits of the Prophet's Companions, chapter 'If I was to take a *Khaleel*', Muslim (2541) in the book of Virtues of the Companions, chapter 'Prohibition of abusing the Companions'. Aboo Daawood (4658) in the book of *Sunnah* chapter 'Prohibition of abusing the Companions', at-Tirmidhee (3860) in the book of Virtues. All from the *hadeeth* of Aboo Sa'eed al-Khudree *(radiyallaahu 'anhu)*. Also reported by Muslim (2540) in the book of Virtues of the Companions in the chapter 'Prohibition of abusing the Companions' from the *hadeeth* of Aboo Hurairah *(radiyallaahu 'anhu)*.

"Indeed Allaah will never unite this Ummah upon misguidance and the Hand of Allaah is upon the Jamaa'ah."[24]

We are pleased with the wives of the Messenger of Allaah (ﷺ), they are the *mothers of the believers* and we believe that they are pure and innocent from all evil.

From the beliefs of the Pious Predecessors is that they do not make it obligatory upon any Muslim to restrict himself to a specific *madhhab*.[25] He can move from one *madhhab* to another, due to the strength of the evidence (in a particular point). The layman has no *madhhab*. Rather his *madhhab* is the *madhhab* of his *mufti* (scholar who gives religious verdicts).[26] If a student of knowledge (*taalibul-'ilm*) has the ability to recognise the proofs and evidences of the Imaams, he should act by it, moving from a *madhhab* of an Imaam, in any issue, to the *madhhab* of another Imaam, due to the strength of the evidence, and the more correct understanding, in an issue. Thus he becomes

---

24. Reported by at-Tirmidhee from the *hadeeth* of Ibn 'Umar (No. 2168) in the book of *Fitan*, chapter 'That which has come in adhering to the *Jamaa'ah*'. Its chain has a weakness, however it has a *shaahid* (supporting narration) with at-Tirmidhee from the *hadeeth* of Ibn 'Abbaas (no. 2167) and another supporting narration with Ibn Abee 'Aasim in *as-Sunnah* (no. 81) from the *hadeeth* of Usaamah bin Shaarik. Thus the *hadeeth* is an authentic *hadeeth*.

25. *Madhhab* is a *school of thought* or a position held by a scholar.

26. Refer to the book *Risaalatul-Taqleed* by Ibn al-Qayyim for it is very important. The layman follows the scholars, as Allaah has ordered him to do in the verse:

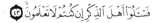

Ask the people of knowledge if you do not know. [an-Nahl (16):43]

The layman by following the scholars is indeed following the Qur'aan and *Sunnah* and not doing *taqleed* (blind following) rather this is called *ittibaa'* for him. However he does not follow the scholars in their mistakes, when it is made clear to him that it is a mistake. This is what is required of the layman, as Ibn al-Qayyim points out in his book.

The one who has the ability to weigh up evidences, ie. a student of knowledge, he can look into the proofs and follow the strongest proof, but the one who does not have the ability, ie. a layman, then he follows the scholars, as Allaah has ordered him to do. (Translator)

Refer also to *Blind Following of Madhhabs*, by Shaykh Muhammad Sultaan al-Ma'soomee (Al-Hidaayah, 1993). [Publisher's note]

a muttabi' (a follower) and not a *mujtahid*.[27] For indeed *Ijtihaad* is the extracting of Islamic rulings from the Book and *Sunnah*, as the four Imaams and others Imaams of the *fiqh* (jurisprudence) and the *muhaddithoon* (scholars of *hadeeth*) have done.

From the beliefs of the *Salaf as-Saalih* is that the four Companions: Aboo Bakr, 'Umar, 'Uthmaan and 'Alee *(radiyallaahu 'anhum)* are the rightly guided *Khulafaa'* and with them existed the *Khilaafatun-Nabuwwah (Khilaafah* upon the Prophetic Way) lasting for thirty years including the *Khilaafah* (ruling period) of Hasan *(radiyallaahu 'anhu)*. This is taken from the saying of the Prophet (ﷺ):

"The Khilaafah in my Ummah is for thirty years then after it is kingship."[28]

From the beliefs of the *Salaf as-Saalih* is that it is obligatory to have *eemaan* (faith) in all that the Qur'aan has come with, and what Allaah, the Most High, has ordered us with, and leaving all that Allaah, the Most High, has prohibited us from, the general and the detailed. We believe in all that the Prophet (ﷺ) has informed us of, when its transmission from him is authentic, in that which we witness or do not witness, regardless of whether we comprehend it, or are ignorant of it or we have not come across the reality of its meaning.

We carry out the orders of Allaah, the Most High, and the orders of his Messenger (ﷺ). We refrain from what Allaah, the Most High, has prohibited us from and what the Messenger of Allaah (ﷺ) prohibited us from. We stop at the *hudood* (boundaries) of the Book of Allaah, and the *Sunnah* of the Messenger of Allaah (ﷺ) and that which has come from the rightly guided

---

27. A *mujtahid* is one who is qualified to extract rulings from the Qur'aan and *Sunnah*, i.e. do *Ijtihaad. (Translator)*

28. Reported by Ahmad in *Musnad* (5/220, 221), at-Tirmidhee (no.2227) in the book of *Fitan*, chapter 'That which has come regarding the Khilaafah', Aboo Daawood (no. 4646 and 4647) in the book of *as-Sunnah*, chapter '*Khulafaa*', Ibn Hibbaan (no. 1534 1535 - in *Mawarid*) in the book of '*Imaarah*, chapter of '*Khilaafah*', al-Haakim in *al-Mustadrak* (3/71, 145) from the *hadeeth* of Safeenah. It is an authentic *hadeeth* and the thirty year period was the period of the rightly guided *Khulafaa* up to when Hasan abdicated from his *Khilaafah*.

Khulafaa. Our duty is to do *ittibaa'* (following) of that which the Prophet (ﷺ) has come with: from beliefs, actions and sayings, to follow the way of Allaah's Messenger (ﷺ), and the four rightly guided *Khulafaa'*, in their beliefs, actions and sayings. This is the complete *Sunnah*, as the *Sunnah* of the rightly guided *Khulafaa'* is adhered to like the following of the Prophetic *Sunnah*.

'Umar bin 'Abdul 'Azeez said:

"The Messenger of Allaah (ﷺ) and the leaders of the Muslims after him set examples (*Sunnah*), the taking of which is holding on to the Book of Allaah, the Most High, and strength upon the *Deen* of Allaah. It is not for any one to change or alter it, nor to look at a matter in opposition to it. Whoever is guided by it then he is truly guided, and whoever seeks help by it then he is truly helped. Whoever leaves it and follows a way other than the way of the believers, Allaah will turn him to what he has chosen and burn him in hell what an evil abode!"

This is confirmed by the saying of Allaah's Messenger (ﷺ):

"....and beware of newly invented matters, for verily every bid'ah is a going astray."

This *hadeeth* is a great principle from the principles of the *Deen* and it resembles another saying of the Prophet (ﷺ):

"Whoever invents in to this Deen of ours that which is not from it, then it is rejected."[29]

In it is a warning from following newly invented matters in the *Deen* and worship. The meaning of *bid'ah* is that which has been invented and has no root in the *Sharee'ah* pointing to it. As for what has a root in the *Sharee'ah* pointing to it then it is not legally (technically) a *bid'ah*; even though linguistically the term *bid'ah* may be applied to it. Thus whenever something new is introduced into the *Deen*, having no root (in the *Deen*) to return it to, then

---

29. Reported by al-Bukhaaree in *ta'leeq* form (without mentioning the chain) (4/298) and in the full form (5/221), Muslim (no.1718), Aboo Daawood in the book of *Sunnah* (no.4606), Ibn Majah (no.14).

it is misguidance - deviation. The *Deen* is free of it, regardless of whether it is connected to issues of beliefs, actions or sayings.

As for the *istihsaan* (approval and condoning) of *bid'ah*, which occurred in the words of the *Salaf*, then that is in relation to *bid'ah al-logawee* (linguistic use of *bid'ah*) and not in the legal (technical) use of the term *bid'ah*. From these saying is the saying of 'Umar bin al-Khattaab, when he gathered the people in *Qiyaam-ur-Ramadaan - Taraaweeh prayers* - behind one Imaam in the masjid. He went out and saw them praying and he said: "What a wonderful *bid'ah*."

This has a root in the *Sharee'ah*. Verily the Messenger of Allaah (ﷺ) prayed it (this prayer) in congregation in the masjid and then left it, fearing that it might become obligatory upon his *Ummah* and that they would be unable to perform it. Indeed they became free of this fear after the death of the Prophet (ﷺ). So 'Umar *(radiyallaahu 'anhu)* revived it. As for that which is a matter confirmed, in worship, then it is not permissible to make additions to it.

So, for example the *adhaan*, remains in the form in which it was legislated, without addition or subtraction. The Prayer remains upon the manner it was legislated as the Messenger of Allaah (ﷺ) said:

"Pray as you have seen me praying."

This is an authentic *hadeeth*, reported by al-Bukhaaree in his *Saheeh*.

Hajj remains upon the manner in which it was legislated, because the Messenger of Allaah (ﷺ) said:

"Take from me your rites (of Hajj)."[30]

Indeed the Muslims have done things that were not present in the time of the Messenger of Allaah (ﷺ), due to them being *daroorah* (necessities) in preserving Islaam. Indeed they have permitted it and kept quiet about it. Like

---

30. Reported by Muslim (no. 1297) in the Book of Hajj.

the gathering of the people to one *mushaf* (that which the Qur'aan is written upon), by Uthmaan bin 'Affaan *(radiyallaahu 'anhu)*, fearing the splitting of the Ummah. Indeed it was approved of by the Companions *(radiyallaahu 'anhum)* and that was for a *maslaha* (benefit).

The example of writing down Prophetic traditions *(hadeeth)* fearing its loss due to the death of its people. The writing of *Tafseer* of the Qur'aan and the Hadeeth. The compilation of *'Ilm-an-Nahw* (science of grammar) to safeguard the Arabic language, which is a means of understanding Islaam. The formation of *'Ilm-al-Mustalah* (science of *hadeeth*). Thus, these are permissible to safeguard the Islamic *Sharee'ah*. Verily Allaah, the Most High, has taken the responsibility of safeguarding His Law - from his saying:

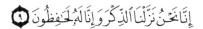

Indeed it is We who have sent down the *Dhikr* (Qur'aan) and surely We will guard it (from corruption).
[al-Hijr (15):9]

The Messenger of Allaah (ﷺ) said:

"This ilm (Deen) will be carried by the trustworthy ones of each generation. Negating from it the tahreef (alterations) of the ones going beyond bounds, the false assumptions of the liars, and the ta'weel (false interpretations) of the ignorant."

This *hadeeth* is *hasan* due to all its chains and *shawaahids* (supporting narrations).

This is the belief *('aqeedah)* - of the first group of this *Ummah* (i.e. the Companions *(radiyallaahu 'anhum)*) and it is a pure belief like the purity of fresh drinking water, strong as the firmly fixed mountains, firm as the firmest of hand holds. It is a flawless *'Aqeedah*, a straight way, upon the methodology of the Book and the *Sunnah* and the sayings of the *Salaf* of this *Ummah* and its *A'immah* (leaders). It is the way which revived the hearts of the pioneers of this *Ummah*.

The Belief of the Pious Scholars of Islaam

It is the *'Aqeedah* of the *Salaf as-Saalih*, *Firqatun-Naajiyah* (saved sect) *Ahl-Sunnah wal-Jamaa'ah*. It is the *'Aqeedah* of the four Imaams[31] - the founders of the well known and followed *madhhabs* and of most of their followers. It is the *'Aqeedah* of the generality of the *fuqahaa*, the *muhadditheen*, the scholars that act on what they know, and those that traverse along their way, to this day and until the Day of Judgement.

Indeed the ones that differed are the ones that altered their (the *imaams'*) sayings, from amongst those of the later generations (*muta'akhireen*) who ascribe to their *madhhabs*.

So our duty is to return, with a pure *'Aqeedah*, to the fountain which the best of our Pious Predecessors drank from. To keep quiet about that which they kept quiet about, to perform our *'Ibaadah* (worship) the way they performed their worship, to adhere to the Book and *Sunnah*, the *ijmaa* of the *Salaf* of this *Ummah* and its *A'immah*, and the correct *qiyaas* in new matters. Imaam an-Nawawee (*rahimahullaah*), said in *al-Adhkaar*:[32]

---

31. Nu'maan bin Thaabit (Aboo Haneefah) - One of the Imaams of Islaam and leading personalities. Born 80 Hijree during the era of the young Companions, he saw Anas bin Maalik (*radiyallaahu 'anhu*) (at a young age). His main students are Aboo Yoosuf and Muhammad al-Hasan ash-Shaybaanee. The *Hanafee madhhab* is ascribed to him but more than a third of the *madhhab* is from other later scholars. He died 150 hijree.

Maalik bin Anas, Imaam of Daar-ul-Hijrah (Madeenah). Born 93 hijree, the year Anas bin Maalik died. An Imaam of the Muslims and a leading scholar of Islaam. The Maalikee *madhhab* is ascribed to him.

Muhammed bin Idrees ash-Shaafi'ee - see footnote (15).

Ahmad bin Hanbal, known as the Imaam of *Ahl-Sunnah wal-Jamaa'ah*. Born in Baghdad 164 hijree. He was from the few who at his time preserved the way of the Companions, fighting away the innovations of the deviant sects and upholding the way of the *Salaf*. From amongst his students were Aboo Dawood, 'Alee bin al-Madanee, Aboo Zu'arah and Aboo Haatim and many more famous scholar of *Ahl-Sunnah wal-Jamaa'ah*. He died 241 hijree.

May Allaah have mercy upon them, they are known as the four well followed Imaams. (Translator)

32. In p137 of my (Shaykh Abdul Qaadir's) checking of *al-Adhkaar* in the book of *Janaaza*, chapter 'What one who is walking with the Janaaza says.'

"...and know that the selected, correct way is that which the *Salaf as-Saalih* were upon, and that is the truth. Do not be fooled by the large number that oppose it. For indeed Aboo 'Alee Fudayl bin 'Iyaad said (the meaning of which is): "Stick to the ways of guidance and you will not be harmed by the smallness of numbers that follow it. Beware of the ways of misguidance and do not be fooled by the multitude of the ones that will be destroyed."

This is the only way that will reform the rest of the *Ummah*. Imaam Maalik bin Anas (*rahimahullaah*), the scholar of Madeenah spoke the truth when he said:

"The latter part of the *Ummah* will never be reformed except by that which reformed the former part."

Never will good disappear from this *Ummah*, because the Messenger of Allaah (ﷺ) said in a *hadeeth*:

"There will not cease to be a group from my Ummah manifestly upon the Haqq (Truth). The ones that abandon them will not harm them, until the Order of Allaah comes and they are like that (upon the Truth)."[33]

The Prophet (ﷺ) further said:

"The example of my Ummah is like that of rain. It is not known whether the initial part (of the rain) is good or the latter part."[34] This is an authentic *hadeeth*.

---

33. Reported by Muslim in his *Saheeh* (no.1920) in the book of *'Imaarah*, chapter 'The saying of the Prophet: *There will not cease to be a group...*' Aboo Daawood (no.4252) in the book of *Fitan*, chapter 'Mention of the *fitnah* and its signs', at-Tirmidhee (no.2177) and (2230) in the book of *Fitan*. All from the *hadeeth* of Thawbaan (*radiyallaahu 'anhu*). The *hadeeth* has various narrations from the *hadeeth* of Mugheerah bin Shu'bah, Sa'd bin Abee Waqqaas, Mu'aawiyyah bin Abee Sufyaan, 'Imraan bin Hussain and others (*radiyallaahu 'anhum*).

34. Reported by Ahmad in *Musnad* (3/130), at-Tirmidhee (no.2873). Also reported in Ahmad (4/319).

Indeed the 'Aqeedah of the Salaf as-Saalih has been stipulated by a great many of the scholars.[35] From them, Aboo Ja'far at-Tahaawee,[36] and his 'Aqeedah has been explained by Ibn Abil-'Izz al-Hanafee[37] one of the students of Ibn Katheer ad-Dimishqee naming it Sharh al-'Aqeedah at-Tahaawiyyah and, from them is Abul-Hasan al-Ash'aree,[38] in his book al-Ibaanah 'an Usool ad-Diyaanah. This being the 'Aqeedah which he finally settled upon. He said: "...our saying, which we state, the Deen which we profess belief in, is adherence to the Book of Allaah, the Sunnah of our Prophet (ﷺ) and that which is related from the Companions (radiyallaahu 'anhum), the Taabi'oon and Imaams of hadeeth, we cling on to this, and we say that which Aboo 'Abdullaah Ahmad bin Hanbal used to say and distance ourselves from ones that opposed his sayings."

---

35. Here it is fitting to mention some of the early books, in which the early scholars have stipulated this pure 'aqeedah:

1. Kitaabul-Eemaan by Abee 'Ubaydah Qaasim bin Sallaam (d.224).
2. Rad 'alaa Zanaadiqa wal-Jahmiyyah by Imaam Ahmad.
3. Rad 'alaa Jahmiyyah by Imaam al-Bukhaaree.
4. Khalq Af'aal al-'Ibaad by Imaam al-Bukhaaree.
5. Al-Eemaan by Ibn Mandah (d.390).
6. As-Sunnah and Usool as-Sunnah by Imaam Ahmad.
7. As-Sunnah by Aboo Bakr bin Athraam (d.272).
8. Kitaab us-Sunnah by 'Abdullaah Ibn Ahmad (d.290).
9. As-Sunnah by Nasr al-Marwazee (d.294).
10. As-Sunnah by al-Khallaal (a student of Imaam Ahmad) (d.311).
11. Kitaab Sharh us-Sunnah By Imaam al-Barbahaaree (d.329).
12. Kitaab ut-Tawheed by Imaam of the A'immah Ibn Khuzaimah (d.311).
13. Al-Ibaanah al-Kubra and al-Ibaanah as-Sughra by Ibn Battah (d.387)
14. Sharh Usool al-'Ittiqaad Ahl-Sunnah wal-Jamaa'ah by Imaam al-Laalakaa'ee (d.418), which is in 9 parts, but printed in 5 volumes, containing the beliefs of the Salaf and many small treatises traced back by isnaad to the Salaf, it is a masterpiece and an essential reference book for all students of knowledge. [Translator]

36. Ahmad bin Muhammed bin Salaamah al-Azdee at-Tahaawee. Died in the year 320 hijree in Egypt and is buried in Qarafa.

37. Abul-Hasan Sadruddeen 'Alee bin 'Alaa-uddeen Ibn Abil-'Izz al-Hanafee. He died in the year 792 hijree.

38. 'Alee bin Ismaa'eel bin Ishaaq from the descendants of Aboo Moosa al-Ash'aree (radiyallaahu 'anhu). Died in the year 323 hijree.

29

From those that wrote about the 'Aqeedah of the Salaf As-Saalih is as-Saaboonee[39] in his book Aqeedat-us-Salaf and Muwaffiq-ud-Deen ibn Qudaamah al-Maqdasee al-Hanbalee[40] in his book Luma'tul 'Itiqaad al-Haadi ilaa Sabeel ar-Rashaad, and other glorious scholars, may Allaah reward them with good.

We ask Allaah to guide us to the pure 'Aqeedah (beliefs) and to a pure and clean heart, we ask for virtuous and pleasing manners, and to give us life as Muslims and to take our life while being upon the Sharee'ah of our Prophet, Muhammad (ﷺ).

O Allaah let us die as Muslims and make us meet the Saaliheen (righteous) without being disgraced or tried. Forgive us, our parents, and the believers on the Day of Judgement. We ask Allaah for inspiration to the correctness of sayings and actions. Indeed He is all powerful over all things and the most worthy to answering calls, and our final du'aa is, all praise belongs to Allaah, Lord of all the worlds.

---

39. Aboo 'Uthmaan bin 'Abdur-Rahman as-Saaboonee, Imaam, Muhaddith, Shaykh-ul-Islaam. He died in the year 449 hijree.

40. Muwaffiq-ud-Deen Aboo Muhammed 'Abdullaah bin Ahmad ibn Qudaamah al-Maqdasee al-Hanbalee. Shaykh-ul-Islaam, a major faqeeh, he died in the year 720 hijree.

GLOSSARY

Adhaan: The call to pray. Its wording is fixed and cannot be altered.

Ahaadeeth: See *Hadeeth*.

Ahkaam (sing. Hukm): An Islamic ruling or regulation.

A'immah: See *Imaam*.

Awliyaa': The friends of Allaah.

Bid'ah: A new matter introduced into the Religion of Islaam having no roots or basis in Islaam; Innovation, and every innovation is reprehensible.

Companion: One who met the Prophet (ﷺ), even if only for an hour or less, believing in him and dying upon Islaam.

Deen: A complete way of life revealed by Allaah; Islaam.

Dustoor: A handbook or manual which one uses to guide oneself.

Daroorah: A necessity which one is compelled into doing.

Faqeeh: A scholar of Islamic law.

Furoo': A subsidiary branch of any matter.

Hadeeth (pl. Ahaadeeth): The action, sayings, characteristics of the Prophet (ﷺ) and silent approvals of the Prophet.

Haafidh: A title given to a scholar engaged in the field of *hadeeth*. The view of the Majority is that it is synonymous to *Muhaddith*.

Hafidhahullaahu: A supplication made for somebody. The meaning is: may Allaah protect him.

Hajj: Pilgrimage to Makkah. One of the five pillars of Islaam which is obligatory upon every Muslim who has the means to perform it.

Hujjah: Acceptable evidence in Islaam.

Hasan: An acceptable *hadeeth* in terms of its authenticity, but does not reach the higher category of *saheeh*.

Ijmaa: Consensus of the Scholars, and it is a subsidiary source of Islamic law.

Ilm: Islamic knowledge.

Imaam (pl. A'immah): A leader, whether in prayer or a leader of a nation, or a leader in knowledge and understanding and this is the more common meaning.

Injeel: The revelation sent to 'Eesa (peace be upon him) which was then corrupted by the Christians after his ascension.

Khalaf: The generations after the first three generations (*salaf*). It also could refer to those who oppose the way of the *salaf*.

Mu'allaq: A *hadeeth* which has had the initial part of the chain of narrators omitted by the one transmitting the *hadeeth*. It is a weak, rejected *hadeeth*. However the *mu'allaq ahaadeeth* in the *Saheehs* of al Bukhaaree and Muslim have special rules.

Mujaddid: A reviver. A scholar who revives the religion of Islaam.

Mujtahid: A scholar who implements *Ijtihaad* to arrive at the Islamic ruling on a specific issue.

Muhaddith (pl. Muhaddithoon): A scholar of *hadeeth*

Muhaddithoon: See *Muhaddith*.

Muttabi': One who follows the evidences upon the understanding of the scholars.

Qiyaas: Analogical deduction of Islamic laws in the absence of texts. New laws are deduced from old laws based on a similarity between their causes. Only resorted to in times of necessity.

Shawaahid: A supporting narration of a *hadeeth* narrated from another Companion.

Saheeh: An authentic *hadeeth*.

Sunnah: A way of conduct. Specifically it refers to the way of the Prophet, and is at times synonymous to *hadeeth*.

Tafseer: Explanation, normally it refers to the explanation of the Qur'aan.

Tawheed: Singling out Allaah, alone for worship of him, and singling out Allaah for his Lordship and Singling out Allaah for His names and attributes.

Tauraat: The revelation sent to Moosa which was then corrupted by the Jews.

Ummah: A community or nation.